7 Water Wonderings

All about the cycle of water.

Heidi Ferris

Other Growing Green Hearts books in this science series:

- 1-2-3 Earth, Air & Me
- Your 4 S's: Senses, Sun, Systems, Seasons
- 5 R's: Rethink, Reduce, Reuse, Recycle, Rejoice*
- 6 C's: Creation, Christ, Creativity, Combustion, Climate, Connect*
- 7 Water Wonderings
- 8 Butterfly Questions

Books that include science and faith together.

Growing
Green Hearts

About This Series

This series of books, Playing with Science & Systems, has been created to be simple, scientifically accurate, and sometimes focused on faith. Science is problem finding and problem solving. The author Heidi Ferris is passionate about encouraging youth to ask questions, boosting science literacy, empowering kids to care for our shared resources, and exploring the wonders in God's creation. Heidi lives in Minnesota with her family - not far from the Mississippi River.

Copyright © 2016 Heidi Ferris, Growing Green Hearts LLC
Written and Edited by: Heidi Ferris
Graphic Design: Lisa Carlson, Spiira Design
Series Consultant: Janine Hanson, Janine Hanson Communications

Contents

7 Water Wonderings

 **Sun shining down on the ground.**

5

6 Surface water all around.

5 Evaporation.

4 Condensation.

10

 # Precipitation on the ground.

13

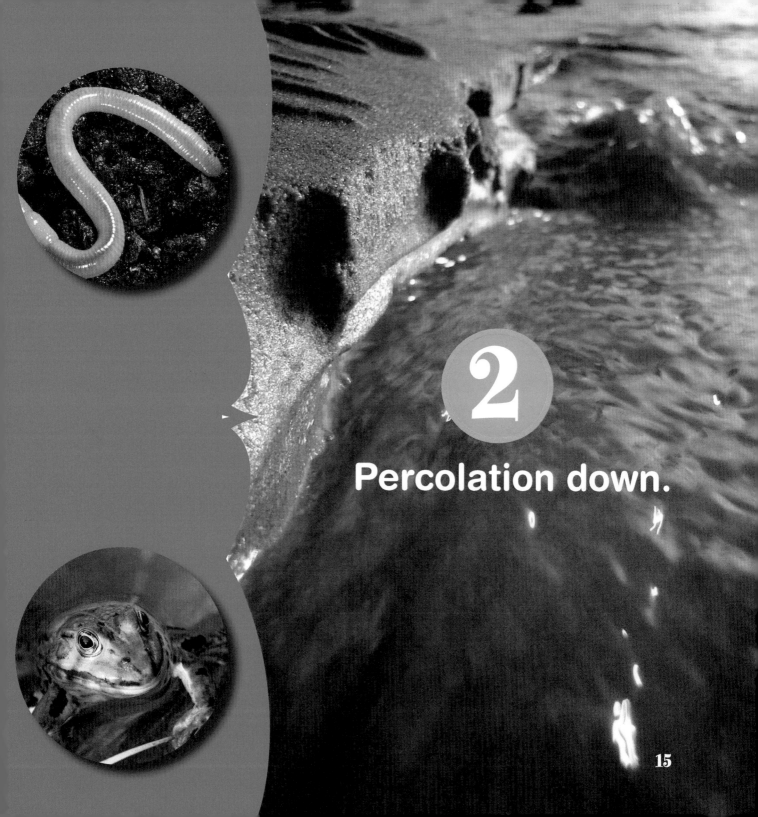

2

Percolation down.

1

Saturation deep underground.

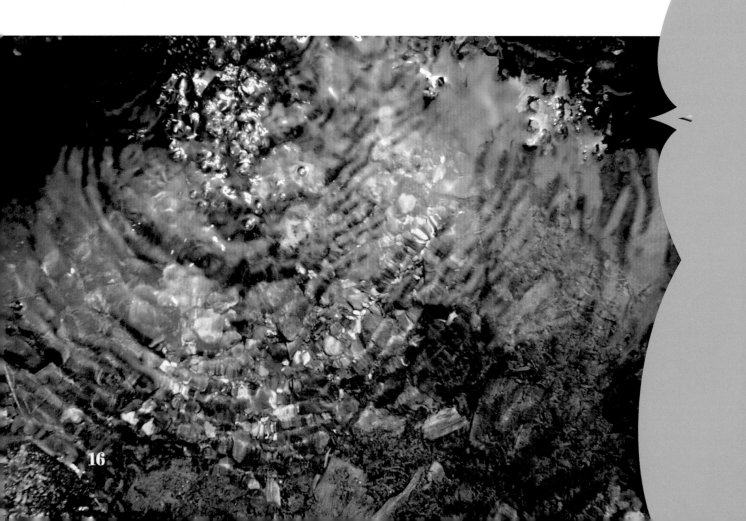

Surface water can trickle down then fill holes in rock deep underground. A well could take those drops back up again into town.

Around and around the water cycle goes. It is not a perfect circle you see... If you are a water drop your path is never that orderly.

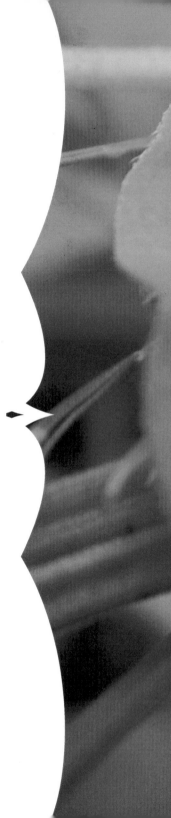

From a street, sink or hose back into nature water eventually goes. Plant roots and rocks way down deep can work to keep water clean. We are a part of the water cycle. Keeping water clean is our job to do too.

Evaporation. Up, up, up it goes into clouds it would seem.

Will drops end up in a puddle, icicle, ocean or stream?

What could be next - a drizzle ride, snowstorm glide or trip into rocks down low? Where the water cycle takes the drops next nobody knows.

Glossary

Water cycle: Water moving around our planet as a liquid, solid, and gas

Evaporation: Heating causes a liquid to change into a gas

Condensation: Cooling down causes a gas to change into a liquid

Precipitation: Water falling from the sky as rain, snow, sleet, hail

Percolation: Water sinking into the ground through sand, soil, or cracks in rock

Saturation: Water has filled the spaces underground and can sink no further

Surface water: Water on the surface of earth such as puddles, snowbanks, rivers, lakes, oceans, wetlands